NEALE ANALYSIS OF READING ABILITY
REVISED BRITISH EDITION

MARIE D. NEALE, OBE

British adaptation and standardization by
Una Christophers *and* Chris Whetton

NFER-NELSON

Neale Analysis of Reading Ability – Revised first published by the
Australian Council for Educational Research, 1988

This edition published by The NFER-NELSON Publishing Company Ltd,
Darville House, 2 Oxford Road East, Windsor, Berkshire SL4 1DF by
arrangement with the Australian Council for Educational Research
Limited.

Printed in Great Britain
ISBN 0 7005 1227 6
Code 2301 02 2
I (7.89)

Contents

Practice Passages

X   for 5–7-year-olds

Y   for 7-year-olds
and above

I have a lot of toys.

I have them in a box.

I like to play with
all of them.

But at bed-time I like
my teddy bear best.

My friend and I made a
tree-house.

We like to hide in it.

We climb up the rope and
pull it up after us.

Then no-one knows where
we are.

We play space-ships.

At tea-time we slide
down fast and we are always
first for tea.

Form 1

Levels 1–6

A bird hopped up to my window.

I gave her some bread.

She made a nest in my garden.

Now I look after her little ones.

Kim stopped on her way to school. In the middle of the traffic lay two children. Their bicycles had crashed into each other. Kim ran quickly to help.

She saw that no-one was hurt. The children pointed to a television camera. 'We are taking part in a road safety lesson,' they said.

As Ali sheltered in an old temple, his shoulder knocked a secret spring. Instantly, he was thrown into an underground room.

In the darkness the walls seemed to be covered with jewels. Ali rested awhile. He knew that desert travellers often imagined strange things.

Later, he explored the place for a way to escape. To his amazement, the jewels were still there. He had found a palace that had been buried long ago.

Jan buckled on her diving belt of metal weights and dropped from the launch. Skipper Kells supervised her air-hose to prevent tangling. Leo, following the bubbles, guided the dinghy above the diver as she searched the mysterious underwater world.

Jan surfaced frequently clutching crayfish. The required number of specimens was almost obtained when the grey nurse shark advanced directly towards her. Jan retreated cautiously without signalling for assistance. The creature brushed by, ignoring her, as baby sharks emerged from some rocky grooves. Their welfare was more important to the shark than the diver's now motionless figure.

Among animals the fox has no rival for cunning.
Suspicious of man, who is its only natural
enemy, it will, when pursued, perform
extraordinary feats, even alighting on the
backs of sheep to divert its scent.

Parent foxes share the responsibilities of
cub-rearing. Through their hunting
expeditions they acquire an uncanny knowledge
of their surroundings which they use in an
emergency.

This is well illustrated by the story of a
hunted fox which led its pursuers to a
neglected mine-shaft enclosed by a circular
hedge. It appeared to surmount the barrier.
The hounds followed headlong, only to fall
into the accumulated water below. The fox,
however, apparently on familiar territory,
had skirted the hedge and subsequently escaped.

Each Spring, at the reappearance of the swallows in their familiar haunts, bird-watchers must marvel at the accurate flights with which birds span the considerable distances between their seasonal abodes. What motivates these regular journeys? The theory that rigorous winters compel birds to migrate is insufficient, as some migrate in summer. Neither can it be argued that the fledglings imitate the older generation, for the offspring generally migrate alone. One reasonable explanation may be that migration is an inborn behaviour, probably originating in the distant past when the flights were essential for survivàl.

Most species favour particular routes. On one occasion when some storks from East Germany were captured and released among storks in West Germany, they did not accompany their relatives along the western migration route. Instead, with unerring instinct, they rediscovered the traditional south-easterly path of their eastern ancestors.

Form 2

Levels 1–6

A black cat came to my house.

She put her kitten by the door.

Then she went away.

Now I have her baby for a pet.

A surprise parcel for Jane
and Peter arrived on Saturday.
Peter looked at the strange
stamps. Jane undid the
string. Then they shouted
with delight. Uncle had sent
some skates for Jane and an
electric train for Peter.
They were what the children
had wanted for a long time.

The lions' final act was in progress.
Jack stood waiting to clear the ring.
The thunder outside the circus tent had made
the lions restless. Suddenly Tina, the
lion trainer, stumbled. Her whip fell.
The youngest lion sprang towards her.

Jack leaped swiftly inside the cage,
cracking the whip with great skill. His
prompt action enabled Tina to regain control
quickly. After that brief adventure, Jack
decided upon his future work.

The fearful roaring of the dragon guided the Knight to the monster's territory. As the intruder crossed the dreaded marshes, the dragon charged furiously, whipping its enormous tail around the legs of the Knight's steed. Horse and rider collapsed.

The Knight now realised that he must attack when the creature was off-guard. He crouched as though wounded. The monster, accustomed to speedy victory, prepared to seize its prey. Then the Knight struck powerfully beneath the beast's outstretched wing. A despairing groan told the villagers that they would be troubled no more.

What excitement to be chosen for a sailing expedition around the world, commemorating the journey of Francis Drake some four hundred years ago!

The young explorers had been selected from different nations for their enthusiasm and range of abilities. The imagination of everyone was stirred. During the long voyage the crew would pursue scientific projects and provide community services.

Their achievements outstripped the dreams of the explorers and their sponsors. Under the direction of scientists the young people salvaged ancient wrecks, rebuilt houses, mapped jungle trails and used aerial walkways to study tall forests. Some overcame physical disabilities to assist in relief work for an area stricken by a hurricane.

Their exploits suggest that courage, adaptability, and the spirit of adventure still flourish.

Realising the necessity to conserve the strength of
the team, the leader decided to pitch an intermediate
camp. The initial enthusiasm and anticipation of
attaining the final camp had been subdued by the
recent mishap in which one member had fallen into a
crevasse. Although the rescue had been accomplished
magnificently, it was obvious that the incident had
hampered the original programme.

The team accepted the leader's decision with relief.
The tedious crawl to the plateau against incessant
winds of varying violence had challenged their
endurance to the limit. Every step at this height
required will-power. Immediately ahead lay an
unforeseen rise from which, by great misfortune,
all the tracks of the advance party had disappeared.
Rest was essential if the team were to withstand the
arduous conditions in the concluding stages of the
assault upon this unconquered peak.

Diagnostic Tutor

Levels 1−3
(2 passages for each Level)
Levels 4−6

Mother gave me a big box.

I put it on the table.

I looked in the box for a toy.

Then out jumped a white rabbit.

I lost my boat.

The wind took it out
to sea.

Then a lost dog went
for it.

Now I have my boat
and a pet dog too.

John and Ann were looking
for tadpoles. Suddenly,
they heard a splash.
A fisherman had fallen into
the lake. He could not
swim because he was hurt.
The children tried to pull
him ashore. He was too
heavy. Then Ann held the
man's head above water,
while John raced for help.

Tony and Susan awoke suddenly. The dog was barking loudly in the yard. The children ran to the window. They could see smoke and flashing lights some way off.

A helicopter had crash-landed in the park nearby. Flames shot into the air. They saw the pilot jump clear and run to safety.

With a soft thud the seagull dropped
to the ground. Black, heavy oil
gripped its wings like glue. Out at
sea oil spread from a damaged tanker.

The stillness of the gull drew Anna
and Nick from their exploration of
the rock pools. The weary gull
cheeped feebly as Anna wrapped it in
Nick's shirt and went for help.
Later the children heard that the
bird had been cleaned at the Zoo,
enabling it to return safely to sea.

It was dusk. Many people had gathered to watch a strange sight. For a while, there was no sign of life on the sand-hills or on the beach.

Then a soft murmur arose from the crowd. Floodlights swept the beach as a line of penguins, bulging with fish for their chicks, came waddling from the surf.

They staggered up the sand-hills along well-worn paths to their burrows. Their chicks thrust their heads out impatiently, and suddenly the wonderful parade had ended.

Dark clouds blotted out the fading daylight. A mournful wailing filtered through the deserted building. The children stopped exploring.

'Ghosts!' whispered one child. 'Nonsense!' replied the other. Nevertheless, they proceeded cautiously in the direction of the mysterious noise.

Gathering courage, and with mounting curiosity, they approached the old kitchen door. Scarcely daring to breathe, they released the catch. Their torches searched the darkness. Immediately their anxiety turned to pity. An exhausted dog lay crouched and whimpering. A gust of wind had slammed the door shut while the dog had been hunting for rats.

The stricken submarine lay at a depth of approximately thirty metres. Although it was common knowledge that the treacherous currents of the area would make rescue operations difficult, the crew remained disciplined and confident.

Meanwhile, outside their prison, a diver with technical equipment for their release was in peril. His lifeline had become entangled around a projection on nearby wreckage. Experience warned him against his first impulse to dislodge the line by force. Patiently he turned and twisted. At last his calmness and persistence were rewarded. Triumphantly he detached the final loop from the obstruction. Then, weary but undaunted by this unpleasant accident, he proceeded to provide an escape exit for the submarine's captives.

The scientists approached the crater's edge fascinated at the prospect of recording the spectacle of a dormant volcano smouldering again. Intent on their photography, they ignored an ominous rumbling. Within seconds, the subterranean cauldron exploded violently, ejecting a great quantity of rocks. Fortunately these fell in the direction of the opposite slope.

Greatly alarmed by this premature explosion, the group hastily began the descent. Immediately, fiery boulders from a gigantic avalanche hurtled around them. Aware that their apparatus hindered progress, they abandoned all equipment except their precious cameras. Then came an anxious moment. As they were evading flying fragments, one of them was struck off-balance by a rebounding boulder. A lengthy halt would have been disastrous. Everyone was, therefore, immensely relieved when they discovered the injuries were superficial. They resumed their hazardous scramble to regain safety just before the surroundings were destroyed.

Extension Passage

It is a curious phenomenon that as technology has become more sophisticated, allowing man to explore beyond the world, there has been a resurgence of wonder and excitement in nature.

Scientific study has illuminated the relationship of life to changing environmental conditions. Sometimes the examples emerge from geological studies, taking us back to the mystery of the Dinosaurs which, 64 million years ago, apparently failed to adapt and became extinct. Yet, prior to that time, for approximately 140 million years, their remarkable adaptability ensured their domination of the earth.

Other knowledge is accumulated from international co-operative endeavours to create sanctuaries for vulnerable species of birds, animals and plants. One example is the rare combination of climate, isolation, sands, marshes, lakes and pine forests which constitute the Coto Doñana National Park in Southwestern Spain. This reserve, which forms a natural conjunction of Africa with Europe, was established by the Spanish Government and the World Wildlife Fund. It is a paradise for the wild geese and other waterfowl as they migrate south from the northern winters. As they fly north again, other species of birds move in from the south.

Along the sea edge, the Plover builds its unprotected
nest in small depressions. In close proximity pure
white dunes of hot sand give shelter to the Viper,
undisturbed except for the predatory swooping of the
Eagle, supreme in the skies. Just inland, and parallel
to the dunes, the pine forests give protection to the
colonies of azure-winged Magpies. In nearby lakes,
from dawn to dusk, the Herons, Spoonbills, Terns and
Flamingos create a kaleidoscope of sparkling colour.
In the scrubland, the Lynx has been assured a habitat
for the perpetuation of its species. Like other
highly valued animals, it had almost been eradicated
through ruthless hunting.

This magnificent museum of unadulterated nature, with
its aesthetic appeal and scientific wonders, is an
eloquent reminder that all countries must learn to
prize their own singular examples of the interdependence
of life.

Supplementary Diagnostic Tests

Detailed directions for using and interpreting the Supplementary Diagnostic Tests may be found in Chapter 5 of the Manual.

Test 1

Discrimination of Initial and Final Sounds

The first test consists of five pictures – an apple, an egg, an insect, an orange, and an umbrella – to test the child's discrimination of the initial and final sounds in a word.

Directions

Say:

> 'Tell me what this picture is.'

If the child does not identify the item, supply the word. Then ask:

> 'Can you tell me just the *first* sound in that word?'

Then point to the group of letters below and say:

> 'Now find which one of these letters down below is the *first* sound in the word?' (i.e. apple).

If the child does not understand the task, use his/her name and demonstrate the initial sound (e.g. M-ark or M-argaret).

Record the child's response on page 7 of the Individual Record, in the space provided for Supplementary Diagnostic Tests.

Then point to the picture again and say:

> 'Tell me the name of this picture again!'

When the child has named the picture, say:

> 'What is the *last* sound you hear in that word?'

Record the child's response.

o l a

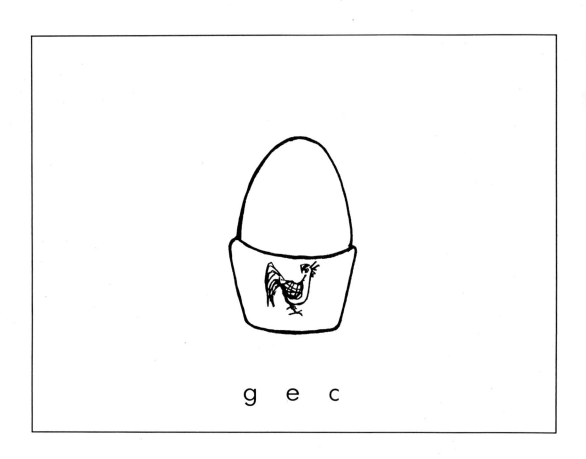

g e c

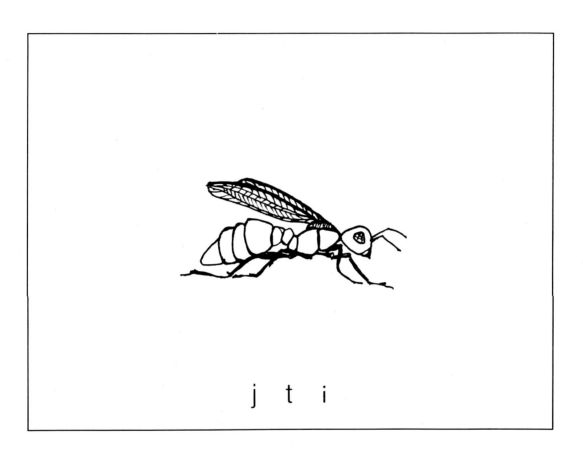

j t i

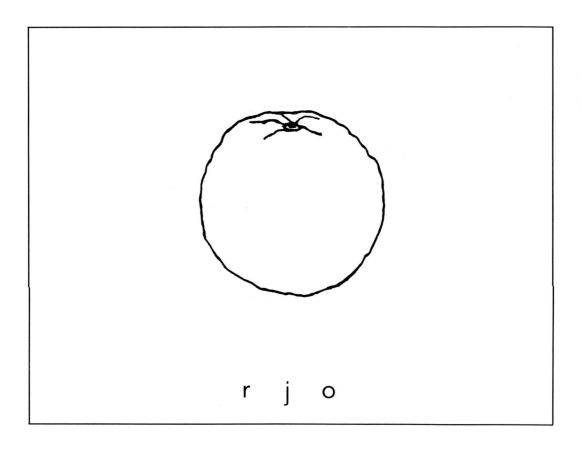

r j o

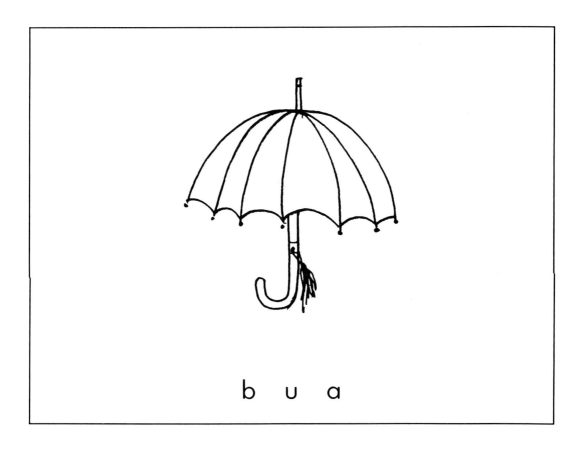

b u a

Test 2

Names and Sounds of the Alphabet

Directions

Say:

> 'What are the names of these letters?'

and point to each letter in turn. As the child proceeds to *name* the letters, say:

> 'Yes. Those are their names: tell me the names of these others,'

and point to the rest of the letters. If the child gives the sound of the letter rather than the name, say:

> 'Yes, but can you tell me their names, for example (pointing to 'a'), **this letter is** *ay.*'

Proceed through the remaining letters. Record incorrect responses in the appropriate place on the Individual Record. Then say:

> 'Now can you tell me the *sounds* that these letters make?'

Accept the sounds that would be consistent with a child's experience of the letter within the initial position of a word, e.g. 'a' for apple.

Mark the errors the child makes in such a way to distinguish errors in letter sounds from errors in letter names. For example, mark errors of naming with a cross and errors of sounding with a circle, as shown below.

p   ✗   Ⓑ   g   ⊗   y

a c o e
f t k h
p d b g q y
m w n r u v
s z x i j l

A H K F E L I T X
C G O Q P R D B J
M N U V Y W S Z

Test 3

Graded Spelling

For this test the child will need a pen or pencil, and some paper to write on.

Directions

Spelling out of Context

You may give the Spelling Test orally by articulating clearly the word for the child to write. Sentence context should *not* be provided. Say to the child:

> 'I want you to write down some simple words. Listen carefully, say the word yourself, and then write it.'

Spelling in Context

Alternatively the Spelling Test may be employed for testing Performance in *spelling-writing* words in context. To do this, you should frame a suitable sentence around the word, to ensure that children have the assistance of meaning to help them with their spelling.
Say to the child:

> 'I want you to write these words. Listen to the word first, then listen to it in a sentence, say the word yourself, and then write it.'

e.g. say:

> 'Cat. I gave the cat some milk.'

The child says 'cat' and writes the word 'cat'.

Items in this list may also be used to test informally the child's blending and syllabification skills.

tap	man	rat
beg	red	pet
tin	lip	ink
fold	bolt	cold
5 but	mug	hutch
show	star	sport
every	bridge	chicken
girl	grid	grumble
light	late	life
10 rice	race	right
gift	gives	gears
taught	called	halt
choice	joints	noise
school	skill	shield
15 several	average	beverage
memory	primary	temporary
combination	congregation	publication
discussion	compassion	destruction
abdominal	abominable	indomitable
20 depreciation	anticipation	negotiation

Test 4

Auditory Discrimination and Blending

Directions for Auditory Discrimination

You will present pairs of words and the child must indicate whether they sound the same or different. Say to the child:

> 'Listen and tell me if the words I say sound the same or different.'

(For example)

> 'jet...............jet..............Are they the same or different?'
> 'plane........train.............Are they the same or different?'

If the child is successful, proceed with the items opposite. If the child does not succeed in the examples, say:

> 'Listen again,' and use the child's name:

(For example)

> 'John ....John' 'Debbie ....Debbie'

Do not proceed with the test if the child fails to make discriminations at this stage.

Directions for Auditory Blending

Items in this list may also be used to test the child's blending skills. Say to the child:

> 'Listen, I am going to say some words that are split up, and I want you to say the whole word.'

(For example)

> 'sh-o-p, shop. Here's another: n-u-t, nut. Here's one more: s-el-f, self.'

Continue with items from the appropriate list on the following page.

Beginning sounds		Medial sounds		Ending sounds	
three	tree	hat	hat	lend	lend
from	from	not	nut	run	rung
sport	sport	pint	paint	task	task
shop	chop	soap	soap	gives	gifts
brick	click	like	look	self	self
still	still	pin	pen	card	cart
scrap	strap	then	than	thump	thumb
dress	dress	gem	gem	sing	sing